The Warm Spirit

Books by Blaine M. and/or Brenton G. Yorgason

The Warm Spirit
Into the Rainbow
Spiritual Survival in the Last Days
Here Stands a Man
Roger and Sybil Ferguson Family History (private printing)
Sacred Intimacy
Little Known Evidences of the Book of Mormon
Decision Point
Pardners: Three Stories on Friendship
In Search of Steenie Bergman (Soderberg Series #5)
KING: The Life of Jerome Palmer King (private printing)
The Greatest Quest
Seven Days for Ruby (Soderberg Series #4)
Dirty Socks and Shining Armour: A Tale from Camelot
The Eleven-Dollar Surgery
Becoming
Bfpstk and the Smile Song (out of print)
The Shadow Taker
Tales from the Book of Mormon
Brother Brigham's Gold (Soderberg Series #3)
Ride the Laughing Wind
The Miracle
The Thanksgiving Promise
Chester, I Love You (Soderberg Series #2)
Double Exposure
Seeker of the Gentle Heart
The Krystal Promise
A Town Called Charity and Other Stories about Decisions
The Bishop's Horse Race (Soderberg Series #1)
And Should She Die
Windwalker (movie version — out of print)
The Windwalker
Others
Charlie's Monument
From First Date to Chosen Mate
Tall Timber (out of print)
Miracles and the Latter-day Teenager (out of print)
From Two to One
From This Day Forth
Creating A Celestial Marriage (textbook)
Marriage and Family Stewardships (textbook)

"Gospel Power Series" by Blaine and Brenton Yorgason

Binding the Lord
The Sword of Testimony
Receiving Answers to Prayer
How to Repent
Satan and His Host
Obtaining Priesthood Power
The Problem with Immorality
Agency, Spiritual Progression, and the Mighty Change
Seeking Wealth
A Gift of Dog Food
To Mothers, from the Book of Mormon
Cory and the Horned Toad

Blaine M. Yorgason

The Warm Spirit

Deseret Book Company
Salt Lake City, Utah

ISBN 0-87579-413-0

Printed in the United States of America

10   9   8   7   6   5   4   3   2   1

The noise in the room with the two suffering babies seemed deafening. Besides their crying and whimpering, between them were an IVAC pump, a kangaroo pump, two cardiac monitors, an oximeter, a pH probe monitor, and a sleep-study machine, each beeping and humming and sounding what seemed like constant alarms to alert the nurses at Primary Children's Medical Center of developing problems. As the piercing alarm on our tiny adopted daughter's cardiac monitor sounded for maybe the tenth time in thirty minutes, indicating that a lead wire had pulled loose again, I rose to my feet in desperation.

"This place is driving me crazy!"

My wife looked at me sympathetically. "I can tell you're upset, dear, but I don't think it's the hospital's fault."

"Maybe, maybe not." I stared out the window as a Life Flight helicopter lifted noisily on its way back to wherever it waited for critically ill little patients, another sign of the pain that surrounded us. Groaning inwardly, I turned back to my wife. "No, it isn't the hospital. In fact, I feel very thankful for it and the doctors and nurses who work here. They're great, and I don't know what we'd ever do without them. It's just that . . . well, I can't take any more of this noise!"

"Where will you go?" Ann asked, not trying to dissuade me. "It's Sunday morning."

"Yeah," I replied, "and Christmas Eve is tonight, so everything is closed. Maybe I'll just go wander the halls here in the hospital."

"The children in the other rooms are just as ill as our baby," she said gently, somehow understanding that it wasn't really the noise that was bothering me.

Slowly I nodded, while tears filled my eyes. "I . . . I just can't bear to see her suffer like this. All this pain just doesn't seem fair! If there was only something I could do. . ."

"Honey," my wife chided softly, "you've given her several priesthood blessings, so you need to leave it to the Lord. Besides, you knew it would be like this when we agreed to bring her into our family. Don't you remember that we both promised, in prayer, that we wouldn't complain, no matter how bad things got?"

I sighed. "I know I agreed, Annie, and I'm not complaining. At least I don't mean to be. I realize that Heavenly Father loves our little girl. But three surgeries in a month? Why doesn't he bless her with a little peace until she goes, either that or take her back right now? Since she's going to die anyway, why does she have to suffer so much?"

For a moment my wife just looked at me, the tears in her own eyes brimming over. At that moment a bustling Santa Claus bounced into the room, wishing us a merry Christmas and leaving a reindeer-crowned candy cane for each of the tiny, unresponsive patients. Moments later he was gone on his merry way, and I was feeling worse than ever.

"Look at that. Our daughter can't even enjoy Christmas! Why, oh why is Heavenly Father doing this to our baby?"

"I don't know," my wife replied softly. "I wish I did . . . But I know Heavenly Father loves her, and I know he loves all these other children here in the hospital. Understanding that, I am just as certain that these little ones and their families will all earn great blessings for what they are going through."

I nodded. "I believe that too, Annie. It couldn't be any other way. I just . . . well, I'm tired of seeing this little angel of ours in so much pain! Day after day, week after week, for sixteen months now. I don't know how much more I can bear to watch her suffer. Do you know she's only had a few good weeks in all that time? If only she would smile again! I can't tell you how much I miss her smile and her cute little giggle.

"Now here it is Christmas, and while millions of children are happily anticipating tomorrow morning's toys, she's stuck here in the hospital without even the mental ability to understand what she's missing. What a lousy place to spend Christmas! What a lousy hand to be dealt in life!"

"You don't really feel like that," my wife said softly, putting her hand on my arm. "I know you don't. I've heard you tell too many people how thankful you are that the Lord honored our family with an eternally celestial child."

I sighed and looked down at our little daughter, who appeared so physically perfect and yet had such great problems. The tube that ran into her nostril was for food, and had been in place since the previous August, when she had somehow lost the ability to suck. Other tubes in her nose were for oxygen, helping her to breathe until the shock of her surgery was past. The wires on her chest and back monitored her heart and respiratory functions, and were the source of the never-ending alarm. Her orange, betadine-swabbed, shaved head, as well as the bandaged incisions on her stomach, indicated that a new shunt had just been installed to drain excess fluid from her head to her stomach cavity. Similar devices had all failed in their operation, and for all we knew, this one would likely fail as well.

Our daughter lay still, but every now and then she would writhe with pain as she whimpered and cried out for relief. The whole scene wrenched my heart more than I could imagine, and knowing that there was no real hope for her mortal future made the situation seem just that much worse.

"Honey," my wife said abruptly, "why don't we both go downstairs to church?"

"But what about little Charity? One of us should stay here with her."

"I'll take care of Charity," a young nurse said brightly as she entered the room. "As a Christmas present, of course. You two go ahead to church. You both look like you could use a break."

"What were you doing?" I grumbled. "*Eves*-dropping?"

She laughed heartily even though she had been rushing from crisis to crisis since seven that morning. She quickly shut off the piercing alarm and began readjusting the lead wires to our baby's chest. "Nurses have 20/20 hearing," she replied as she worked. "That's part of our training. Now hurry, or you'll be late."

I smiled weakly and thanked her. Then my wife and I gave a longing look at our tiny daughter and departed for the bottom floor of the hospital where the LDS services were being held.

As we walked down the long hallway to the elevator, we passed room after room of critically ill children. In one room a child who was battling leukemia sat playing a game with his mother. He was hairless, but he was also smiling, so at least the nausea from his chemotherapy was gone. Two rooms that we passed were isolation rooms where the children were suffering with RSV, respiratory syncytial virus, which led to bronchiolitis. Highly infectious, these isolated children seemed to be in a great deal of pain. In another room lay a tiny girl who had been born with ventricular ceptal defect, a hole in the lower chamber of her heart. She had also been born without corneas in her eyes, and there was much urgency as the staff tried to ready her heart so she could have the strength to undergo cornea transplant surgery. There were also children who suffered from gastroenteritis and meningitis (which Charity was also suffering from, in addition to her holohydrencephalus) and various traumas caused by accidents of one sort or another. In fact, one entire unit in the hospital was the multiple trauma unit, where children with multiple organ injuries from accidents, abuse, and so forth, were cared for.

But doing all within their power to solve all these problems were the nurses and doctors — dozens and dozens of dedicated men and women who each seemed to have a special way with children. For Charity there was a host of nurses and volunteers

5

who, even when they were not assigned to Charity, would go out of their way just to hug her or kiss her and say hello. Charity affected people that way. Almost totally limited in her ability to interact either physically or mentally with others, still she radiated through the crystal-clear blue prisms of her eyes a peace and love that was perhaps the most contagious disease in the hospital.

Thus our daughter was monitored constantly by teams of physicians from neurosurgery, neurology, and gastroenterology. But Charity's condition puzzled them all. She was a tiny, pain-bound but eternally celestial, enigma. Her agony seemed never to diminish for longer than a few days no matter what was done medically, and both the doctors and we were beginning to doubt that she would ever know *any* peace again.

Stepping to the side of the hall, we smiled as a group of carolers moved slowly past us, their words ringing into the rooms of the suffering children: "Hark! the herald angels sing/ Glory to the new-born King!"

"Isn't it wonderful that people are willing to give so much for others?" Ann asked as we continued down the hall. "Look at those carolers. They don't have to be here, and this is about as unresponsive an audience as they could find. Yet here they are, all dressed up and singing like the angels they represent. This is really touching, don't you think?"

Silently I nodded.

"I admit that it's hard to see all this suffering," Ann observed as we walked along, skirting a Christmas fairy and several scurrying nurses. "But I'll say one thing—I don't think we could ever find more caring people than those who labor here."

"Or braver parents," I added as we stepped aside for a mother who was maneuvering her wheelchair-bound child and an IV stand toward us. "I can't get over how young most of these parents are. I don't think I could have handled this when I was younger. In fact, I'm not even sure I can handle it now!"

Ann looked at me but said nothing, the woman with the child and the IV smiled and wished us a merry Christmas, and moments later we entered the gaily decorated elevator. But I wasn't thinking of Christmas decorations as we descended. Instead I was pondering the young mother's seasonal wishes and bright countenance, wondering where she had managed to find such coverage.

We had never attended the Sunday service at Primary Children's Medical Center before, and I watched the proceedings with interest. A specially called PCMC branch president conducted the meeting under the authority of a member of a local high council, but the mother of a patient led the singing — all Christmas hymns that day. A sister of another patient played hymns on the piano, a young patient offered the invocation, two young fathers of very ill babies blessed the sacrament, and a young deacon wearing an awkward-looking brace stood with his visiting older brother to pass the sacrament once the prayers had been given.

Watching all these people giving service, I thought of the pain each of them was covering up but still feeling — pain I had never imagined existed until Charity came into our family — and suddenly I realized that I was weeping.

Now, I have a tendency to weep anyway when my heart is full, at least a little. But this was different — very different.

For one thing, I could not stop. I could not even slow it down. For another, my chest felt as though it were on fire, and I was quaking or trembling visibly, something else I could not stop.

"Are you all right?" Ann whispered anxiously as she took my hand.

I nodded, fumbling for my handkerchief. "I . . . I feel such an unusual outpouring of the Spirit."

Scant moments later my wife wiped at her own eyes and squeezed my hand. "I feel it too," she whispered. "The only other time I ever felt like this was that day in the temple . . ."

She stopped speaking, for she had no need of going further. I too was remembering the experience, perhaps the most sacred moment in our lives, a moment that had come after a lengthy period of great difficulty and much fasting and prayer, a brief hour when both of us had felt an incredible outpouring of the Holy Ghost. In fact, in the dozens of times we had discussed it since, we had both concluded that being in the actual presence of Jesus Christ would surely feel something like what we had felt that day.

Now we were experiencing that same overwhelming feeling, but with a difference. In the temple the experience had been for me and my wife, as a result, I had always believed, of our faith and efforts at repentance. In the hospital, however, I had the feeling that we were simply bystanders, witnesses of some sort of spiritual phenomenon that had more to do with the patients in the hospital than it did with us. I didn't understand what was happening, but over the years I have come to accept a great deal of what I don't understand — accept, enjoy, and move onward. And that's what I decided to do then.

After the service we returned to the fifth floor, discussing our experience as we slowly climbed the stairs. The intense spiritual feeling had lasted at least thirty minutes, and then, just as suddenly as it had come, it had gone. We marveled that we should have been allowed to share that sacred experience, and, alone once again with our suffering little Charity, we gave silent thanks that the Lord had allowed the power of the Spirit to be in the hospital that day.

• • •

Later I sat in the cafeteria, eating alone so that my wife could remain with Charity. As I took my first bite, I noticed a young man watching me. He was an employee, a dishwasher I thought, and I knew that he was mentally handicapped.

Oh, no, I thought as I saw his sober gaze resting on me. *I hope he doesn't want to sit with me. I don't feel like making up a conversation with someone like him. Not today. There is so much that I want to think about, to ponder.*

I watched furtively and was relieved when he finally sat at the next table. Slowly I continued to eat, but I could tell that he wasn't eating. Even without looking I knew that he was simply waiting, watching me. He hadn't even touched his food.

Come on, I grumbled at him in my mind. *Just eat your dinner. Can't you tell that I want to be left alone?*

Still the young man said nothing; he just watched me. So I took another bite, and as I did so, from out in the hall came the sounds of another group of Christmas carolers:

I heard the bells on Christmas day
Their old familiar carols play,
And wild and sweet the words repeat
Of peace on earth, good will to men.

As I listened to the song, from out of nowhere a voice inside me spoke. "What's the matter with you?" I was asked rather abruptly. "Don't you believe in Christmas?"

Sure I do, I mentally answered in surprise.

"Then why don't you act like it?" the voice inside me questioned. "You enjoyed a marvelous spiritual experience this morning, wherein the Lord spoke great peace to your soul. Where is your 'good will' to men that you cannot reach out and speak peace to the soul of another?"

I . . . uh . . .

"Did you think that the Spirit came only to bless and comfort you and the physically ill?" the voice persisted. "Did you think that, outside of the little children, you and Ann were the only ones who felt it? You know very well that Jesus suffered in order that he might bring comfort to his innocent ones, his children, no matter what their age or why they are suffering. And just as your little Charity will always remain pure and innocent, so also is this young man who is watching you one of the truly innocent."

I . . . I hadn't thought of it quite like that, I stammered to myself.

"You need to," I was told just as quickly. "And you need to repent while you're at it. After all, this is Christmas. If Heavenly Father and his Beloved Son could send forth the

Holy Spirit on a Christmas visit to all these children, and if seeing pain in these innocent ones is as distressing to you as you have been claiming, then couldn't you perhaps give a little time and love to one who must suffer much longer than your Charity will ever suffer—a little 'peace on earth, good will to men'?"

Encompassed by great guilt, I slowly nodded my head.

Suddenly the voice inside me became gentle again. "Besides, my friend, you have always loved Christmas. Here is a chance to make this one just a little bit better than any you have yet enjoyed."

Feeling terrible, I solemnly apologized to heaven for my arrogance. Then, with the beginnings of a genuine smile, I turned to meet the gaze and welcome the amazing friendship and Christlike love of one of the Savior's truly elect on this earth.

•   •   •

"Are you alone?" he asked the instant my gaze met his. His face was gravely serious.

I nodded.

"Can I eat with you?"

I hesitated briefly but then nodded my agreement. He stood up quickly, picked up his tray, and stepped to my table.

"My name's Fred," he told me as he carefully arranged his tray and sat down. "What's your name?"

I told him.

"That's a good name," he said sincerely. "I have a warm spirit. Want to feel it?"

Surprised at his question, I wondered how to respond. After all, I knew that this young man was mentally deficient, at least to some extent. But he was also very polite, and though he had not smiled even once, which seemed a little strange, my inclination was to treat him as I would any other adult. But his question —

"You say you have a warm spirit?" I asked.

"Uh-huh. Want to feel it?"

"Sure," I replied, trying not to grin. "Only, how do you feel —" But before I could finish my question, Fred reached out and clapped his hand on my forehead.

"See how warm my hand is?" he asked matter-of-factly. "That's because of my warm spirit."

For a moment I sat in startled silence, almost stunned by the incredible warmth of Fred's hand on my head. It was warm, almost hot, but definitely not unpleasant. For a moment I wondered how my own hand would feel —

"Do you have a warm spirit?" he asked as he suddenly pulled his hand away, almost as if he had read my mind.

"I . . . I don't know. I . . . "

"Here," he said, reaching out and taking my hand in his. "Put it on my head, and let me feel."

I let my hand be guided to his head. He held it still for a few seconds and then let go. "It's a little warm," he declared as he took his first bite of food. "Not as warm as mine, though. Do you know why mine is so warm?"

I shook my head.

"Because I love people," he said simply. "Love is what makes my spirit warm."

"How do you know that?" I asked, remembering my struggle to even want to visit with him.

"My bishop told me. Are you glad it's Christmas?"

"I am," I responded. "I love Christmas."

"Me too. Does that hurt? It looks like it hurts a lot. I'll bet it does, doesn't it?"

Glancing down, I saw that Fred had his fingertip pointed at the blackened nail of my left forefinger, smashed months before between two heavy cans of wheat. I was startled that he had noticed it, but even more startled at the genuine concern and even pain that filled his voice.

"No," I quickly told him, "it doesn't hurt. It did once, but no more."

"Oh, that's good," he breathed with relief. "I hate to hurt. I fell once and hurt my head. It was awful. My bishop says I have limitations. Do you know what limitations are?"

Once again caught off guard, I struggled to formulate an answer. "Uh . . . why don't you tell me," I finally suggested.

Fred nodded agreement. "Limitations are when I can't do all the things that other people do," he stated quickly. "That's why I don't hold the priesthood. I have limitations here in my head. But my bishop told me that as long as I have a really warm spirit, I won't ever need the priesthood, at least while I'm alive. Then after I die I can have it. Does the bus go past your house?"

"Uh . . . the bus? No, I . . . uh . . . "

"I have an apartment of my own, and I ride the bus up

13

here to work. When I hurt my head it was because I fell off the step of the bus. It was slick. Does that hurt?"

Again I looked down to where he was pointing, and this time Fred had spotted a small scab on my other hand, a scab I had not even noticed. He touched it gently with his forefinger. "No," I replied as I shook my head in wonder. "I don't even remember hurting it."

"That's good," he said again, with definite relief sounding in his voice. "It isn't fun to hurt. My bishop says that if I can keep my warm spirit, after I die I won't ever hurt again. If a warm spirit is caused by love, why isn't your spirit as warm as mine?"

I don't think I even answered him that time. The question was too direct, too abrupt, and the answer was too painful.

"Here," he said, sensing my discomfort, "let me feel your spirit again. See? It's getting warmer—a little. My bishop says that means you are getting more love. Do you have someone in the hospital you are visiting?"

"Yes," I replied as I pulled my hand back to feel it for the warmth that I truly hoped was there. "My baby daughter is upstairs. She . . . has limitations too. In fact, when she was born, Heavenly Father didn't give her all she needed in order to live. Now she is slowly dying."

"Then she has a really warm spirit, doesn't she."

"Yes," I said quietly, "I suppose she does."

"Did you know that Jesus has the warmest spirit of all?"

"I . . . hadn't ever thought of it like that."

"He does. My bishop told me so."

More and more I was admiring the wise counsel of this

young man's bishop, a church leader who was performing a wonderful labor, not only with Fred but, through him, with others.

"You love your bishop, don't you," I said.

"I love everybody," Fred replied simply.

I didn't know how to respond to such a sweeping declaration of righteousness, especially when it was made with such absolute sincerity. So I did the only thing I could do; I changed the subject.

"What do you like best about Christmas?"

Fred looked at me as though contemplating an answer, though I was soon to learn that such was not the case. Instead he threw me another curve.

"Did you know that Jesus came to the hospital today?" he finally asked.

"Huh? I mean . . . Jesus what?"

Fred gazed at me soberly. "Jesus came here to the hospital," he finally stated again, very matter-of-factly. "For Christmas. Before today, I thought he only went to the temple. I'm going to go to the temple after I die. My bishop says I will have a wife after I die, and even little children. That's because I won't have limitations anymore. Why do you think Jesus came here to the hospital?"

"Uh . . . why would you think?" I asked, for the first time in the conversation seeing no recourse but to take the offensive.

"Oh," he said, still very serious, "I already told you, but I just wondered if you heard. He came because it's Christmas, and he wanted to wish us 'Merry Christmas.' He came down here in the kitchen to see me too, you know."

15

"He did?" I asked, no longer surprised by anything this young man might say. "How do you know?"

"Because he wouldn't ever forget me. He loves me. He is my friend. Besides, my spirit is very warm today. I think when he came to see me and wish me 'Merry Christmas,' he gave me some of his warm spirit to help mine be warmer. If the bus ever comes to your house, can I come to see you?"

"Why . . . uh . . . certainly," I replied, still trying to comprehend Fred's simple but incredibly great faith. "I'd like that."

For a moment or so Fred ate in silence, but I ate nothing. I believe I toyed with my food a little, but my mind was racing too much to eat. Jesus had come to the hospital. Jesus had come to the —

Suddenly I sat straight with realization. Jesus had come to the hospital! The incredible outpouring of the Spirit that my wife and I had felt during the church service — might that have been one and the same event?

"Fred, what time did Jesus come?"

"A little while ago," he answered after clearing his mouth of food. "This morning. This is good gravy."

I nodded agreement, but my mind was still scrambling, trying to believe that what my wife and I had experienced might have been an actual visit by the Savior of the world. That took a real stretch for my faith, but as I worried the idea like a dog worrying a bone, I suddenly realized that a scripture was going through my mind, around and around as though it were on a spinning drum. The scripture declared, "Mine eyes are upon you. I am in your midst and ye cannot see me."

Now, abruptly, I realized that the Holy Ghost had brought

that scripture to my mind. Just as abruptly, I found myself truly believing that we really had been in Christ's presence, for the burning and the trembling and the weeping — the overwhelming emotion of love I had felt — had been so transcendent that I could not imagine it being caused by any other thing.

When I started to ask myself why Christ had visited the hospital, instantly, once again through the inspiration of the Holy Ghost, my mind was filled with the answer. My tears started flowing all over again. And the answer was as Fred had already told me. What my sweetheart and I had experienced, I now knew, had been a tender visit by the Savior of the world to some of his sweet, pure, little innocent ones who were suffering so much pain on this eve of the day marked on the calendar as his birthday. Surely on this Christmas he was in the midst of them, as the scripture said, yet for the most part we "whole" people had known it not.

"Do you know why I believe Jesus came?" I asked Fred in a broken whisper.

"Why?" he asked soberly.

"If I am right, then I think he came because he understands my little daughter Charity's pain — hers as well as the pain of the rest of his innocent ones who are here, including you — and he weeps with their suffering just as I weep."

Fred watched me and said nothing.

"That is why only his suffering, innocent ones were recipients of his visit."

Fred remained silent.

"How he must long for the world to finally accept him, and to become pure enough to be in his presence all the time. Only then will we all be allowed to feel that joy; only then will all of this pain and suffering finally be done away with—"

"I'm very careful on the steps of the bus," Fred stated suddenly, as though I hadn't even been speaking. "That's because I don't want to hurt my head anymore. I'll be careful when I come to see you. Are you through eating?"

I nodded.

"I can't go upstairs where the babies are, but I can walk up and down the hall. Can I walk to the bottom of the stairs with you?"

I nodded again, we picked up our trays, and in silence we handed them through the window to the dishwasher. Then we turned and walked down the hall to the foot of the stairs.

"Would you let me shake your hand?" Fred asked as we paused.

Eagerly I took his hand and was surprised at the firmness and warmth of his grip.

"Can I shake your other hand?"

Somewhat awkwardly I shook his other hand.

"Your spirit is getting warmer," he said, encouraging me along just as I used to encourage my children when they were small. "Can I have a hug?"

Silently I nodded, and so Fred put his arms around me and pulled me close. Then he held me, his cheek pressed tightly against mine. After what seemed to me a long time, he pulled away and looked at me.

"Your spirit is much warmer than it was. When you hug me, does it make you nervous?"

"Why?" I asked, feeling guilty because it had.

"Some people don't like to hug. They think it is bad. But they don't have warm spirits. I like you a lot. Can I have another hug?"

We hugged again, shook hands twice more, and, still without a smile, Fred told me that he loved me. That was when I decided to ask him.

"Fred, do you ever wish you didn't have . . . limitations? I mean, do you ever think you got handed a raw deal in life? Don't you get tired of things being so hard all the time?"

His countenance very serious, Fred regarded me in silence. In fact, he was quiet so long that I wondered if he had even understood my questions. I was about to ask them again, using different words, when he finally responded.

"When I hurt my head, I told my bishop that hurting was very hard. He told me that when things got hard for me, it just meant that Jesus loved me lots."

"But wouldn't Jesus want to help you — to stop your pain?" I asked, forgetting for a moment that I was speaking with a young man who knew Jesus personally.

"Hurting does help me," Fred answered with absolute certainty. "It helps me to feel like Jesus felt when he hurt. My bishop said that Jesus had hard things happen to him just like me, and that I should be happy I have been blessed to be like him. That's why I'm happy. I'm always happy!"

"And . . . your limitations?" I pressed. "Don't you wish you didn't have them?"

"If I didn't have limitations," Fred declared patiently, making sure that I understood, "I wouldn't have such a warm spirit. That would make it much harder to be Jesus' friend. I'm happy

19

I'm his friend, because today he came to see me and wish me 'Merry Christmas.' "

Then, without another word, Fred turned and walked away. Silently I stood watching him, trying my best to sort out the incredible array of emotions I was experiencing. Fred was happy in his limitations; he did not think he had been given a raw deal. And suddenly I knew that, if I could have spoken with my tiny daughter, she would have told me the same thing!

Filled with rejoicing, I was just turning to hurry up the stairs to rejoin my wife and celestial daughter when Fred spun back to face me.

"Someday when the bus comes to your house," he called out from halfway down the hall, "I will come to see you. Then I can feel your little girl's warm spirit, and she can feel my warm spirit. She has limitations like mine, so Jesus must love her a lot, just like he loves me. I'll bet he came to wish her 'Merry Christmas' today too."

"Yes," I replied softly, "he did. In fact, he came here to wish 'Merry Christmas' to everybody, including even me, and to give each of us his Christmas gift—a warm spirit.

"Thank you, Fred, for helping me to unwrap mine."

Author's Note

Although the preceding story is fictional, it is based on actual events and actual people who work at Primary Children's Medical Center. During the 1989 Christmas season, my wife, older children, and I were privileged to spend several days at that hospital, where our baby daughter, Charity Afton, was a patient. I say privileged because, by being at PCMC during the Christmas season, we were witness to many beautiful and heart-warming acts of kindness and concern.

Born severely defective in mortal body, Charity is unable to respond to life in the same manner as more "normal" children. Her problems are considered terminal. Yet not once during that stay, or any of her fifteen other stays at PCMC, have we encountered any feeling other than complete support and concern for our baby daughter's needs. She has been loved, cuddled, cared for, and fussed over by doctors, nurses, and other members of the hospital staff, as well as by community members who regularly serve the patients there, just as we try to do for her ourselves.

Despite the pain and suffering that have occasioned each of our celestial daughter's hospital visits, we as a family are deeply thankful to all of the PCMC family for their unceasing love and concern. In behalf of little Charity Afton, we thank them sincerely.

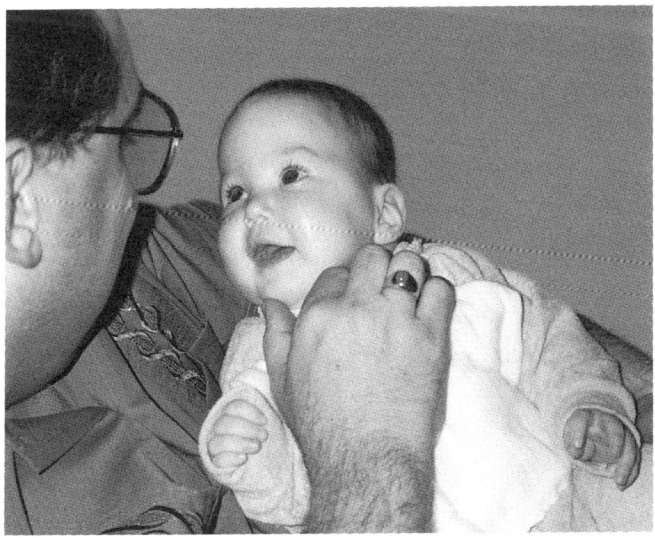

The author, Blaine M. Yorgason, and his daughter, Charity Afton Yorgason